Here's One I Wrote Earlier
Year 3

Here's One I Wrote Earlier

Instant resources for modelled and shared writing

Year 3

Gill Matthews and Gill Howell

Learning Matters

First published in 2001 by Learning Matters Ltd.

British Library Cataloguing in Publication Data
A CIP record for this book is available from the British Library.

ISBN 1 903300 24 X

Cover and text design by Topics – The Creative Partnership
Project management by Deer Park Productions
Typeset by Anneset, Weston-super-Mare, Somerset
Printed and bound in Great Britain by Ashford Colour Press, Gosport, Hants.

Learning Matters Ltd
58 Wonford Road
Exeter EX2 4LQ
Tel: 01392 215560
Email: info@learningmatters.co.uk
www.learningmatters.co.uk

Contents

Introduction

Here's One I Wrote Earlier, as its name suggests, offers a substantial bank of examples of writing that you can use in modelled and shared writing sessions.

Demonstrating how to approach a particular piece of writing, or an aspect of the writing process, is an extremely effective teaching strategy. However, to think of ideas and to prepare resources for these sessions can be time consuming – and often challenging.

The examples provided here range from brief character portraits to complete playscripts, from non-fictional recounts to adventure stories. These examples are at different stages of development – from planning, to an outline draft version and then to a polished frame – so you can use them to take children through the whole writing process.

What are modelled and shared writing?

Modelled and shared writing take place during the whole-class session of the literacy hour. They are used to demonstrate specific skills and strategies used by writers. Modelled writing involves the teacher in 'creating' the piece of writing in front of the class. Shared writing is collaborative – the children make suggestions for content, choice of vocabulary, sentence construction, etc.

Children often think that experienced writers write perfectly all the time. It is important therefore when using both teaching strategies, that you talk to the children about how you write e.g. rehearsing sentences out loud before writing them down, explaining choices of particular words and phrases, discussing possible spelling options. It is useful sometimes to make mistakes and to demonstrate how to edit and improve a piece of writing as you write.

To keep the children interested during modelled and shared writing, you could involve them by using interactive techniques e.g. asking questions, giving quick individual writing tasks on the whiteboard, taking time out for discussions, asking the children to come out to the front to write. Make sure that all the children can see – and reach – the writing surface. When appropriate, write on paper rather than a wipe-clean surface as this will mean the writing can be returned to for further work.

How to use this book

There are two ways to find appropriate writing examples in this book:

- Page v lists the contents of the book by literacy focus. Use this page to find, for example, samples of dialogue or instructions.

- The grid on page ix lists the teaching objectives covered and the relevant examples of writing.

The examples are organised by term and in groups that take you through the development of a piece of writing. **All the examples in the book may be photocopied.** Some examples have been annotated so you can use them to focus on specific teaching points (for example, pages 3 and 6, 23, 44, and 48, etc.).
Each page is organised in the same way to help you find your way around each example quickly and easily. Each example is prefaced by contextual information and is linked clearly to the National Literacy Strategy (NLS) teaching objectives.

You'll also find suggested writing activities after each example:

 This indicates suggestions for teacher-led activities when working with the whole class.

 This indicates suggestions for activities the children could complete independently, either on their own, in pairs or in groups.

You may wish to remove the activities section at the bottom of the page and then enlarge the page, or make copies for use on an OHP. In some instances, you could give copies to the children for them to work on independently. Equally, you could use them for ideas and present them as if you had written them earlier!

Stimulus material

Wherever possible, the topics chosen for writing for each term have been linked to provide continuity. The examples are based on the identified range of texts for reading and writing in the NLS *Framework for teaching,* and some non-fiction writing has links to other curricular areas e.g. a science or history topic from the same, or earlier, term. Traditional tales and rhymes are used frequently as these provide a well-known basis that allows the children to focus on the writing process rather than be diverted by unfamiliar or challenging content.

Planning grid

To aid planning, this grid refers to word, sentence and text level teaching objectives in the NLS Framework for teaching.

Term 1

Word level	Page	Sentence level	Page	Text level	Page
4	16, 17	3	2, 3	9	15
19	2, 3	7	1, 3	10	2, 3
		8	1, 3	11	4, 5, 6, 7, 8, 9
		9	11, 13	13	15, 16, 17
		11	4, 5, 6, 7, 8	14	10
		12	4, 5, 6, 7, 8	15	11, 12, 13, 14
		13	1	16	3
				22	18, 19, 20
				23	21, 22, 23, 24

Term 2

Word level	Page	Sentence level	Page	Text level	Page
		2	28	6	29, 30, 31, 32
		9	42, 43, 44	7	29, 30, 31, 32
		10	42, 43, 44	8	25, 26, 27, 28
				9	33, 34, 36, 37, 38, 39
				10	33, 34, 35
				11	40, 41
				16	42, 43, 44

Term 3

Word level	Page	Sentence level	Page	Text level	Page
13	47, 48	2	49, 50	10	45
		4	47, 48, 49, 50	11	46, 47, 48
		5	57, 58, 59, 60	12	49, 50
				13	45
		6	57, 58, 59, 60	14	51, 52
				15	53, 54
				20	57
				22	55, 56, 57, 58, 59, 60
				23	57
				25	55, 56

Term 1 Fiction

Dialogue
Main focus Speech punctuation (see also pages 2 and 3)
NLS teaching objectives S7, S8, S13

What can I get you?

I would like 10 fish and chips, 15 fish, chips and peas, 7 sausage, gravy and chips and 9 portions of curry sauce.

OK, that will be quite a few minutes. Have you got visitors?

Umm . . . yes, they just dropped in out of the blue.

Oh, are they all relatives?

No, I don't think so. They don't look like Mum.

Are they your Dad's relatives then?

Maybe . . . but he only drives a car. This lot turned up in a space ship!

Well, I hope they like fish and chips!

Activities

- Add appropriate speech punctuation.
- Draw attention to the use of capitals to mark the start of direct speech and to the use of a new line for a new speaker.
- Discuss how we know there are two characters and who is speaking.
- Draw attention to the use of commas in lists.

- Add speech verbs and character names.

Term 1 Fiction

Dialogue
Main focus Speech verbs
NLS teaching objectives W19, S3, T10

"Hello again," said Elvis, "how did the aliens like the fish and chips?"

"They went down very well," said Joe.

"What can I get you today?" said Elvis.

"Nothing. Can you come with me?" said Joe. "They are waiting just outside."

"What?" said Elvis.

"They need to meet you," said Joe.

"Why?" said Elvis.

"Well, they said something about you opening a fish and chip shop on Mars," said Joe.

"Me?" said Elvis. "Just give me a minute and I'll go and pack!"

Activities

- Replace the verb 'said' with more interesting and powerful speech verbs.
- Discuss and explore how varying the position of the speech verbs adds interest to dialogue.

- Write a short dialogue for the future meeting between Elvis and the alien leader.

Term 1 Fiction

Dialogue
Main focus Annotated model text (see also pages 1 and 2)
NLS teaching objectives W19, S3, S7, S8, T10, T16

Speech marks around spoken words

"What can I get you?" asked Elvis.

Use of commas in lists

"I would like 10 fish and chips, 15 fish, chips and peas, 7 sausage, gravy and chips and 9 portions of curry sauce," replied Joe.

New line for each change of speaker

"OK, that will be quite a few minutes," answered Elvis. "Have you got visitors?"

"Umm ... yes, they just dropped in out of the blue," Joe muttered.

Punctuation before closing speech marks. Can be ,.!?

"Oh, are they all relatives?" Elvis enquired.

"No, I don't think so. They don't look like Mum," said Joe.

"Are they your Dad's relatives then?" questioned Elvis.

Speech interrupted mid-sentence by speaker's name. Lower case letter used to restart speech.

"Maybe," Joe grinned, "but he only drives a car. This lot turned up in a space ship!"

"Well, I hope they like fish and chips!" Elvis exclaimed.

****

"Hello again," smiled Elvis, "how did the aliens like the fish and chips?"

Varied position of speech verbs

"They went down very well," Joe replied.

Variety of speech verbs

"What can I get you today?" asked Elvis.

"Nothing. Can you come with me?" urged Joe. "They are waiting just outside."

"What?" gasped Elvis.

"They need to meet you," pleaded Joe.

Clear use of proper nouns

"Why?" gulped Elvis.

"Well, they said something about you opening a fish and chip shop on Mars," whispered Joe.

"Me?" cried Elvis. "Just give me a minute and I'll go and pack!"

Activities

- Use as a model to demonstrate how to write dialogue.
- Use a variety of speech verbs and accurate speech punctuation.

Term 1 Fiction

Familiar settings A fish and chip shop
Main focus Improving a draft
NLS teaching objectives S11, S12, T11

One day, a boy went into a fish and chip shop. It was hot inside. There was a queue. He stood in it. The man behind the counter was very busy. The shop was noisy and smelly. The boy waited.

Prompt questions

1. When did this happen?

2. Who is the main character?

3. What time of day was it?

4. How can we show the time of day?

5. What could the main character see?

Hear?

Smell?

Feel?

Activities

- Use this draft for demonstrating how to write settings.
- Use the prompt questions to develop an improved version through shared writing.
- Revise use of capital letters and full stops to punctuate sentences.

- Use the planning frame on page 9 to draft a paragraph describing a setting.

Term 1 Fiction

Familiar settings A fish and chip shop
Main focus Model text (see also page 6)
NLS teaching objectives S11, S12, T11

It was late one Friday afternoon. The setting sun shone

on the steamy windows of McGill's fish and chip shop.

Joe stood patiently in the queue. He watched Elvis

hand the neat, paper-wrapped parcels to the

customers. He could hear a basket of chips sizzling in

hot fat. The smell of vinegar and frying food filled the

shop. Joe held his list and money tightly as he waited.

Activities

- Use as a model to demonstrate how to write descriptions of settings.
- Focus on the use of the senses to create the sense of the setting.

Term 1 Fiction

Familiar settings A fish and chip shop
Main focus Annotated model text (see also page 5)
NLS teaching objectives S11, S12, T11

It was late one Friday afternoon. The setting sun shone — When

on the steamy windows of McGill's fish and chip shop. — Where

Joe stood patiently in the queue. He watched Elvis
— Who

hand the neat, paper-wrapped parcels to the

customers. He could hear a basket of chips sizzling in — Use of senses

hot fat. The smell of vinegar and frying food filled the

shop. Joe held his list and money tightly as he waited.

Activity

- Use as a model to demonstrate how to write descriptions of settings.

Term 1 Fiction

Familiar settings The playground
Main focus Improving a draft
NLS teaching objectives S11, S12, T11

The teacher was in the playground. It was noisy. There were lots of children. It was autumn so there were lots of leaves. Someone had a bonfire. The teacher blew her whistle to tell the children to line up.

Prompt questions

1. Where did this happen?

2. Who is the main character?

3. What season was it?

4. How can we show the season?

5. What could the main character see?

Hear?

Smell?

Feel?

Activities

- Use this draft for modelled writing.
- Use the prompt questions to develop an improved version through shared writing.

- Use the planning frame on page 9 to draft a paragraph describing a setting.

Term 1 Fiction

Familiar settings The playground
Main focus Model text
NLS teaching objectives S11, S12, T11

Mrs Berg stood in the playground and listened. She could hear shouting and laughter as children chased the leaves that blew around. She watched as others crunched and kicked through red and gold heaps. She could smell smoke from a nearby bonfire. She blew her whistle and the sounds of playtime stopped.

Activity

 • Use as a model to demonstrate how to write descriptions of settings.

Term 1 Fiction

Familiar settings Planning frame
Main focus Making notes
NLS teaching objective T11

1. When did this happen?

2. Who is the main character?

3. What time of day was it?

4. How can we show the time of day?

5. What could the main character see?

Hear?

Smell?

Feel?

Activities

 • Use the planning frame to demonstrate how to make notes about a familiar setting.

 • Use the planning frame to make own notes about a familiar setting.

Term 1 Fiction

Writing calligrams Trees
Main focus Model text
NLS teaching objective T14

T

Hand leaves
Hand leaves
Have branches

R

Hand leaves
Hand leaves
Have branches

Hand leaves
Hand leaves
Have branches

E

Hand leaves
Hand leaves
Have branches

E

S

And roots
And roots
And roots
And roots

Activities

- Use as a model to demonstrate how to design and write calligrams.
- Discuss other suitable subjects for calligrams.

Term 1 Fiction

Playscripts Humpty Dumpty
Main focus Improving a draft
NLS teaching objectives S9, T15

Humpty Dumpty: Help! Help! I'm stuck up here on the wall. I think I'm going to fall off! Ouch! That really hurt.

The King's Men: You silly egg. Why were you sitting on the wall? We'll try to put you back together again.

Humpty Dumpty: I don't think you'll be able to, I have broken into millions of little pieces.

The King's Men: Well, we'll try.

Prompt questions:

How do we know who is talking?

How easy is it to understand what is happening?

How could we make what is happening clearer?

What could happen next?

Activities

- Use the prompt questions to improve the draft version.
- Focus on the use of italics to identify the speaker.

- Continue the playscript.

Term 1 Fiction

Playscripts Humpty Dumpty
Main focus Completed planning frame
NLS teaching objective T15

1. Characters
Humpty Dumpty
King's Horses and King's Men
Old Man

Do I need a narrator? Yes

2. Setting
Wall with good view of the countryside

3. Beginning
HD decides to climb on wall
Spends ages admiring view
Sees lots of men on horses (King's Horses and Men)

4. Middle (problem)
Falls off wall
Breaks into pieces. Can't be mended

5. Ending
Old man comes along
Puts him back together by magic
HD promises never to climb on walls again

Activities

 • Use as a model to demonstrate how to plan a playscript (see page 14).

 • Begin to develop plan into a playscript.

Term 1 Fiction

Playscripts Humpty Dumpty
Main focus Model text
NLS teaching objectives S9, T15

The Fall of Humpty Dumpty

Narrator: An egg called Humpty Dumpty decided that he would like to see what was on the other side of a really high wall at the bottom of his garden. He climbed onto the top of the wall and sat staring at the view.

Humpty Dumpty: Wow! I can see for miles and miles. I didn't know this beautiful countryside was on the other side of the wall.

Narrator: Humpty spent hours sitting on the wall, gazing at the countryside. Suddenly he saw something.

Humpty Dumpty: What is that? I can see a lot of people on horses! It's the King's Horses and the King's Men! Yoohoo! Hello! Can you see me?

Narrator: Humpty got very excited and started wriggling about and shouting.

Humpty Dumpty: Hello, Hello! King's Men! Can you see me? It's Humpty up here on the wall!

Narrator: Humpty started to wobble on top of the wall and then he slowly toppled off onto the ground below.

Humpty Dumpty: Ouch, that really hurt! Oooh my head!

Narrator: Humpty had broken into tiny pieces.

The King's Men: You silly egg. Why were you sitting on the wall? We'll try to put you back together again.

Activities

- Use as a model to demonstrate how to write a playscript. Focus particularly on the layout e.g. use of characters' names before their speeches.
- Discuss how the narrator is used to tell the story.

Term 1 Fiction

Playscripts Planning frame
Main focus Making notes
NLS teaching objective T15

1. Characters

Do I need a narrator?

2. Setting

3. Beginning

4. Middle (problem)

5. Ending

Activities

 • Use the planning frame to demonstrate how to make notes for a playscript.

 • Use the planning frame to make own notes for a playscript.

Term 1 Poetry

About the senses I Saw
Main focus Model stimulus
NLS teaching objectives T9, T13

I Saw

I saw a peacock with a fiery tail
I saw a blazing comet drop down hail
I saw a cloud with ivy circled round
I saw a sturdy oak creep on the ground
I saw an ant swallow up a whale
I saw a raging sea brim full of ale
I saw a Venice glass sixteen foot deep
I saw a well full of men's tears that weep
I saw their eyes all in a flame of fire
I saw a house as big as the moon and higher
I saw the sun even in the midst of night
I saw the man that saw this wondrous sight.

Anon

Activities

- Focus on the rhythm of the lines (10 syllables per line) rather than the rhyming pattern.
- Brainstorm ideas for a class poem about sight or other senses.
- Use the structure of the poem to develop an alternative version through shared writing or use the version on page 17 for modelled writing.

- Draft a poem about another sense using this poem as the basis (see also page 16).

Term 1 Poetry

About the senses I Heard
Main focus Improving a draft
NLS teaching objectives W4, T13

I Heard

I heard a bird chirping at dawn
I heard a star falling to earth
I heard snow landing on a path
I heard flowers opening in the sun
I heard a baby laughing at his mum
I heard the earth settling down to sleep
I heard an ice cream van driving up the road
I heard the wind blowing round my house
I heard a crowd cheering at a goal
I heard mums talking in the playground
I heard the TV on in an empty room
I heard trees dropping leaves.

Activities

- Focus on the sounds that can be heard and those that can't.
- Count and discuss the number of syllables in each line.
- Start to improve the poem by making each line contain 10 syllables (see also page 17).

- Improve the poem by making each line contain 10 syllables.

Term 1 Poetry

About the senses I Heard
Main focus Model text
NLS teaching objectives W4, T13

I Heard

I heard a blackbird welcoming the dawn
I heard a shooting star falling to earth
I heard soft snowflakes landing on a path
I heard a flower blossoming in the sun
I heard a baby laughing at his mum
I heard the old earth settling down to sleep
I heard an ice cream van drive up the road
I heard a mighty wind blowing round my house
I heard a crowd cheering as their team scored
I heard mums chattering in the playground
I heard the TV in an empty room
I heard a tree drop its leaves in autumn

Activities

- Use as a model to demonstrate how to write simple patterned poems.
- Discuss the use of 10 syllables in each line, the use of the repeated opening phrase and the use of imaginative words and phrases.
- Draw attention to the mix of some sounds that can be heard and others that can't (see also page 16).

Term 1
Non-fiction

Reports Hedgehogs
Main focus Model text
NLS teaching objective T22

Brown   Worms   Caterpillars and beetles

Hibernates November to March

Poor eyesight   26 cms long

Weighs up to 1100 gm   Towns and cities

Spines 25 mm long

Good sense of smell and hearing

Can swim and climb   **HEDGEHOGS**   Mammal

Cat and dog food   Water not milk

Babies called hoglets   Nests in leaves

Noisy eaters

Five claws on each foot

Woodland,   country in fields

Gardens   5000 – 7000 spines   Gardener's friend

Activities

 • Use as a model to demonstrate how to brainstorm.

 • Group information according to individually developed criteria on a concept map (see page 19).

**Term 1
Non-fiction**

Reports Hedgehogs
Main focus Concept map framework
NLS teaching objective T22

What they look like

Brown,
Spines 25mm long
five claws on each
foot
5000-7000 spines

Where they live

Woodland
in fields, gardens
towns and cities

HEDGEHOGS

Interesting fact

What they eat

Water not Milk.
Worms
cater

- Use as a frame for grouping similar information under relevant headings.

- Use to start grouping similar information in preparation for planning and writing a report.

19

Term 1
Non-fiction

Reports Hedgehogs
Main focus Model text
NLS teaching objective T22

A report about hedgehogs

Introduction
Mammals

What they look like
Brown
Spines 25 mm long
Adults 26 cm long, weigh up to 1100 gms
Poor eyesight, good sense of smell and hearing
5 claws on each foot

Where they live
Cities, towns, country, woodland, gardens.
Hibernate November to March in dry leaves.

What they eat
Gardener's friend.
Beetles, worms, caterpillars.
If humans leaving food out — cat/dog food. Water not milk
Noisy eaters

Interesting facts
5000–7000 spines
Babies called hoglets
Group of hedgehogs called a prickle

Activities

- Use to demonstrate how to organise facts under relevant headings.
- Begin to use facts to create a draft report (see page 21).

- Continue to create a draft report.

Term 1
Non-fiction

Reports Hedgehogs
Main focus Improving a draft
NLS teaching objective T23

A report about hedgehogs

Introduction
Hedgehogs are mammals.

What they look like
Hedgehogs are brown. They are covered in spines. The spines are 25 mm long. Adult hedgehogs are about 26 cm long and can weigh up to 1100 gms. Hedgehogs have poor eyesight but they do have good senses of smell and hearing. Hedgehogs have five claws on each foot.

Where they live
Hedgehogs live in towns and cities. They also live in the country and woodland. They live in gardens in towns and in fields in the country. The hibernate from November to March. They build their nests in dry leaves.

What they eat
Hedgehogs are called the gardener's friend. They eat insects like beetles. They also eat worms and caterpillars. If humans want to leave food out for hedgehogs they will eat cat or dog food. Water is better to leave out than milk. Hedgehogs are very noisy eaters.

Interesting facts
Hedgehogs have between 5000 and 7000 spikes. A group of hedgehogs is called a prickle.

Activities

- Use to demonstrate how to structure a report.
- Demonstrate how to improve a draft (see page 22).

Term 1
Non-fiction

Reports Hedgehogs
Main focus Model text (see also page 23)
NLS teaching objective T23

Hedgehogs

Hedgehogs are small mammals.

Hedgehogs are covered in brown spines that are about 25 mm long. They have between 5000 and 7000 spines. Hedgehogs have poor eyesight but they do have good senses of smell and hearing. They have five claws on each foot so their footprints are quite easy to identify. Adult hedgehogs are about 26cm long and can weigh up to 1100 gms.

Hedgehogs live in towns and cities as well as in the country. They can often be seen in gardens. Hedgehogs hibernate from November to March. They build their nests in dry leaves, often under garden sheds and bonfires.

Hedgehogs are called the gardener's friend because they eat insects like beetles. They also eat worms and caterpillars. If you want to feed hedgehogs, leave cat or dog food out for them. Milk upsets their stomachs so only give them fresh water to drink. You may hear a hedgehog feeding as they are very noisy eaters.

A group of hedgehogs is called a prickle.

Activities

- Use as an example of the structure of a report.
- Use as a model to demonstrate how to improve a draft.

Term 1 Non-fiction

Reports Hedgehogs
Main focus Annotated model text (see also page 22)
NLS teaching objective T23

Hedgehogs

Definition — Present tense

(Hedgehogs are small mammals)

Hedgehogs (are) covered in brown spines that are about 25mm long. They (have)

between 5000 and 7000 spines. Hedgehogs have poor eyesight but they

do have good senses of smell and hearing. They have five claws on each

foot so their footprints are quite easy to identify. Adult hedgehogs are

about 26cm long and can weigh up to 1100 gms.

What they look like

Technical vocabulary

Hedgehogs live in towns and cities as well as in the country. They can

often be seen in gardens. Hedgehogs (hibernate) from November to March.

They build their nests in dry leaves, often under garden sheds and bonfires.

Where they live

Hedgehogs are called the gardener's friend because they eat insects like

beetles. They also eat worms and caterpillars. If you want to feed hedgehogs,

leave cat or dog food out for them. Milk upsets their (stomachs) so only give

them fresh water to drink. You may hear a hedgehog feeding as they are

very noisy eaters.

What they eat

Technical vocabulary

A group of hedgehogs is called a prickle. ————— Interesting Fact

Activity

- Use as a model to demonstrate how to write a report.

Term 1
Non-fiction

Reports Planning frame
Main focus Making notes
NLS teaching objective T23

A report about:

Introduction	
What they look like	
Where they live	
What they eat	
Interesting facts	

Activities

 • Use the planning frame to demonstrate how to make notes for a report.

 • Use the planning frame to make own notes for a report.

Term 2 Fiction

Character portraits Big Bad Wolf
Main focus Making notes
NLS teaching objective T8

Character's name: Big Bad Wolf

What does Big Bad Wolf look like?
hairy
big eyes
big, brown long, pointy ears
shining, white teeth
wet, pink tongue

What kind of person is Big Bad Wolf?
shifty
cunning
always hungry
scheming

How does Big Bad Wolf move?
quickly
nippily
scampers
creeps
skulks

How does Big Bad Wolf talk?
growls
wheedles
whispers
shouts

Activity

- Use the plan as a model to demonstrate how to make notes about a familiar character (see also page 26).

Term 2 Fiction

Character portraits Planning frame
Main focus Making notes
NLS teaching objective T8

Character's name _____

What does _____ look like?

What kind of person is _____ ?

How does _____ move?

How does _____ talk?

Activities

- Use the planning frame to demonstrate how to make notes about a familiar character.

- Use the planning frame to make own notes about a familiar character.

26

Term 2 Fiction

Character portraits Big Bad Wolf
Main focus Organisation and language
NLS teaching objective T8

FOR SALE

1 wolf, answers to the name of BB. Long, silky fur. Big, brown eyes. Shining, white teeth. Wet, pink tongue. Healthy appetite.

Fast mover, often blends into the background.

Does good imitations. Not suitable for homes with children or old ladies.

Phone: Forest 1234.

Ask for Mrs R. Hood.

Activities

- Demonstrate how to use notes (from page 25) to create a character portrait.
- Draw attention to the organisation and brevity of the language.

- Use as a model for own writing.

Dear sir,

I would like to apply to join your band Wolflife.

I think I have the right looks for a pop band. I have brown, shiny hair, big eyes, shiny teeth and a wet nose. I am a very funky mover and can soon learn new dance steps. I can creep and scamper better than most wolves of my age.

I have a strong voice that can be low or quite high. I can even impersonate females. I use my brains and could become involved in planning the band's future. I am hungry for success.

I look forward to hearing from you.

Yours sincerely,

BB Wolf

Activities

- Demonstrate how to use notes (from page 25) to create a character portrait.
- Draw attention to the use of adjectives.
- Experiment with changing some of the adjectives and the impact this has.

- Use as a model for own writing.
- Use the planning frame (page 26) to plan and write a character profile that describes the ideal member of the band 'Wolflife'.

Term 2 Fiction

Story planning Little Red Riding Hood
Main focus Making notes (version 1) (see also page 30)
NLS teaching objectives T6, T7

Characters:

Little Red Riding Hood — little girl, dressed in red, kind and helpful (good character)

Big Bad Wolf — cunning (bad character)

Setting:

Forest
Grandma's cottage

Beginning:

Red Riding Hood in forest, on her way to take food to her grandma.

Wolf sees her and wants to eat her.

Tricks her into telling him where she is going.

Wolf runs quickly to Grandma's cottage and eats her.

Problem:

Red Riding Hood arrives at Grandma's cottage.

Wolf pretends to be Grandma.

Red Riding Hood notices Wolf's eyes, ears and teeth. Realises it is not Grandma.

Ending:

Woodcutter cuts open Wolf and Grandma escapes.

Activity

- Use the plan to demonstrate how to make notes about a story.

Term 2 Fiction

Story planning Planning frame
Main focus Making notes (version 1) (see also page 29)
NLS teaching objectives T6, T7

Characters:

Setting:

Beginning:

Problem:

Ending:

Activities

- Use the planning frame to demonstrate how to make notes for a story.

- Use the planning frame to make own notes for a story.

Term 2 Fiction

Story planning Little Red Riding Hood
Main focus Making notes (version 2) (see also page 32)
NLS teaching objectives T6, T7

Beginning
Who?
Little Red Riding Hood
Big bad Wolf
What?
Little Red Riding Hood skipping through forest.
Wolf following her, hiding behind trees.
Why?
Little Red Riding Hood taking food to grandma
Wolf wants to eat her.

Problem
Who?
Wolf, dressed up as Grandma.
Little Red Riding Hood
What?
Wolf lies in bed, pretending to be Grandma.
Little Red Riding Hood doesn't realise it is the Wolf at first. Then notices Wolf's big eyes, ears and teeth and realises it is not Grandma in the bed.
Why?
Wolf is trying to trick Little Red Riding Hood.

Ending
Who?
Wolf
Little Red Riding Hood
Woodcutter
What?
Woodcutter rescues LRRH by cutting open Wolf. Out steps Grandma.
Why?
Good beats evil

Activities

- Use the plan to demonstrate how to make notes about a story.
- Discuss the last point – good beats evil as a story theme.

Term 2 Fiction

Story planning Planning frame
Main focus Making notes (version 2) (see also page 31)
NLS teaching objectives T6, T7

Beginning

Who?

What?

Why?

Problem

Who?

What?

Why?

Ending

Who?

What?

Why?

Activities

 • Use the planning frame to demonstrate how to make notes for a story.

 • Use the planning frame to make own notes for a story.

Term 2 Fiction

Alternative versions of traditional tales Little Red Riding Hood
Main focus Completed plan
NLS teaching objectives T9, T10

Beginning

Who?
Little Red Riding Hood
Big bad Wolf
What?
LRRH skipping through forest, Wolf following her.
Why?
LRRH taking vegetables to village fete to enter in tastiest vegetable competition.
Wolf wants to steal vegetables to enter in competition himself.

Problem

Who?
LRRH
Wolf
What?
Wolf dressed up as judge of vegetable competition.
LRRH doesn't realise it is Wolf at first. Then notices big eyes, ears and teeth and realises it is Wolf.
Why?
Wolf trying to trick LRRH into giving him the vegetables.

Ending

Who?
LRRH
Wolf
Grandma
What?
Grandma trips up Wolf and wraps him in knitting wool.
Why?
Good beats evil

Activity

 • Use as a model to demonstrate how to plan an alternative version of a traditional tale.

Term 2 Fiction

Alternative versions of taditional tales Little Red Riding Hood
Main focus Drafting
NLS teaching objectives T9, T10

Once upon a time, Little Red Riding Hood was skipping through the forest taking some vegetables to the village fete. She was going to enter them in the tastiest vegetables competition. The Wolf had his eye on Red Riding Hood. He wanted to steal the vegetables and enter them in the competition himself.

Red Riding Hood arrived at the village hall. She waved at Grandma who was waiting for her. A large figure trotted towards Red Riding Hood. 'Do give me your vegetables my dear,' said the figure to Red Riding Hood, 'I'll take them into the hall for you.' Red Riding Hood looked at the figure. 'Who are you?' she asked.

'I'm the judge of the tastiest vegetables competition,' replied the figure. Red Riding Hood looked closely at the judge.

'What big eyes you have,' she said.

'All the better to see the vegetables with,' he said.

'What big teeth you have,' she said.

'All the better to taste the vegetables with,' he said.

'What big ears you have,' she said.

'All the better to hear the vegetables with,' he said.

'You can't hear vegetables!' shouted Red Riding Hood. 'You aren't a proper judge at all. You are the Wolf!'

The Wolf ran off but suddenly fell flat on his face as Grandma stuck out her foot. Quick as a flash, Grandma tied him up with her knitting wool. Red Riding Hood was able to enter the vegetables in the competition and they won first prize.

Activities

- Use as a model to demonstrate how to turn a plan into a draft.
- Discuss the similarities and differences between this version and the original.

Term 2 Fiction

Alternative versions of traditional tales Little Red Riding Hood
Main focus Alternative endings
NLS teaching objective T10

As the Wolf lay in Grandma's bed, Red Riding Hood couldn't help noticing his rather trendy clothes.

'What a lovely shirt, Grandma,' she said.

'All the better to dance in,' the Wolf replied.

'What lovely shoes, Grandma,' said Red Riding Hood.

'All the better to dance in,' the Wolf replied.

'What lovely music, Grandma,' said Red Riding Hood as a catchy tune began playing in the kitchen.

'All the better to dance to,' said the Wolf leaping from the bed.

Red Riding Hood screamed, 'You aren't my Grandma!'.

'No,' answered the Wolf, 'but I can dance better than she can!' And with that, the Wolf grabbed Little Red Riding Hood and whirled her around the cottage. They danced and they danced and they danced until Red Riding Hood was quite worn out.

'Oh, Wolf!' she gasped, 'you are a wonderful dancer.'

'I know,' agreed Wolf, 'you aren't too bad yourself. A bit of practice and we could become champions.'

Red Riding Hood and Wolf practised night and day. At the next forest disco dancing championships they won the first prize and continued to do so year after year after year. And they both lived happily ever after.

Activity

 • Use as a model to demonstrate how to write an alternative ending to Red Riding Hood.

Term 2 Fiction

Adaptations of myths How the spider got eight legs
Main focus Planning
NLS teaching objective T9

How the spider got eight legs

Characters
Spider — very helpful creature with four arms and legs

Setting
Jungle

Beginning
Spider very busy — lots of jobs to do. Trying to help so many other creatures.

Problem
Can't get all jobs done.
Decides needs more hands.
Grows four more arms.

Ending
Spider is a hard and fast worker because she has eight arms and legs.

Activities

- Use the story plan (page 30) to model planning a myth.
- Discuss the fact that myths attempt to explain how or why something happened.

Term 2 Fiction

Adaptations of myths How the spider got eight legs
Main focus Model text
NLS teaching objective T9

How the spider got eight legs

Once long ago, reader, in the deepest, darkest jungle, Spider was a hard working creature. She was particularly good at helping to keep places clean.

As she became more well known for her hard work, more creatures asked for her help. She worked harder and harder until one day she felt completely exhausted.

Lion came to see her: 'Can you help with our spring cleaning?' he asked.

'I'm really too tired,' Spider answered.

Giraffe came to see her: 'Can you help with our spring cleaning?' he asked.

'I'm really too tired,' Spider answered.

Zebra came to see her: 'Can you help with our spring cleaning?' he asked.

'I'm really too tired,' Spider answered.

'You have been working too hard,' said Zebra.

'I know,' replied Spider, 'but I can't let people down. I just don't have enough hands to do all the jobs I'm asked to do.'

Zebra laughed. 'You need another pair of hands,' he said.

Spider sat in her web and thought, 'Zebra is right, I do need another pair of hands. In fact I need two more pairs of hands.'

Spider went to visit Cheetah, the wisest of the jungle creatures, and asked how she could get two more pairs of arms. Cheetah said, 'It sounds as though a bit of magic is called for.' He gave Spider some magic powder and told her to roll in it once a day.

Spider followed Cheetah's instructions and, three days later, when she woke up she had grown two more pairs of arms. Now she could do ever so many jobs all at once. Ever since then, spiders have had eight arms and legs.

Activity

 • Use as a model to demonstrate writing an alternative myth.

Term 2 Fiction

Adaptations of fables The hare and the tortoise
Main focus Planning
NLS teaching objective T9

The hare and the tortoise

Characters
Hare
Tortoise

Setting
Hare's kitchen
Beginning
Hare challenges tortoise to a cooking competition. Asks fox to be judge.

Problem
Hare finishes first and eats what he has cooked

Ending
Fox can only taste tortoise's food so tortoise is the winner

Moral
Fastest is not always best

Activities

- Use as a model (see page 39) to demonstrate how to complete a plan for an alternative fable.

- Use the headings to plan an alternative fable.

Term 2 Fiction

Adaptations of fables The hare and the tortoise
Main focus Model text
NLS teaching objective T9

The hare and the tortoise

One day a hare was teasing a tortoise. 'You are so slow and clumsy,' he said, 'I bet I could beat you in any kind of competition, even a cooking competition.'

'I don't think you could,' said the tortoise.

'OK, I challenge you to a cooking competition,' said the hare. 'We'll each cook something and we'll ask the fox to judge whose food tastes the best.'

The next day all the animals met in hare's kitchen. 'Ready, steady, go!' said the fox. Hare and tortoise started cooking. Hare rushed around banging pots and pans and making a terrible mess. His food was soon ready and he started to tidy up. 'I'm feeling really hungry after all that cooking,' he said. He looked at tortoise's cooking, 'Your food won't be ready for ages,' said hare. He thought he would just have a little taste of his own food 'Oh, that tastes wonderful,' he said and tasted a little bit more and a little bit more. Finally, tortoise announced that he had finished.

'Now for the judging,' announced the fox importantly.

Hare looked at the few crumbs left on his plate and then at tortoise's tasty-looking food. 'Oh dear,' said hare, ' I don't seem to have anything left.'

'Then I declare that tortoise is the winner,' said fox.

Moral: Fast is not always best.

Activity

• Use as a model to demonstrate how to write an alternative fable by improvising on an existing fable.

Term 2 Poetry

Performance poems Chicken and Chips
Main focus Model
NLS teaching objective T11

Chicken and Chips

Chicken and chips,
Chicken and chips,
Everybody here likes
Chicken and chips.

We eat them all day,
Never throw them away,
We all like chicken and chips.

Choc ice and chips,
Choc ice and chips,
Everyone here likes
Choc ice and chips.

We eat them all day,
Never throw them away,
We all like choc ice and chips.

Chop suey and chips,
Chop suey and chips,
Everyone here likes
Chop suey and chips.

We eat them all day,
Never throw them away,
We all like chop suey and chips.

Chips and chips,
Chips and chips,
Everyone here likes
Chips and chips.

We eat them all day,
Never throw them away,
We all like chips and chips.

Anon

Activity

- Use as a model to demonstrate how to improvise on a poem (see page 41).

Term 2 Poetry

Performance poems Bacon and Eggs
Main focus Writing new verses
NLS teaching objective T11

Bacon and Eggs

Bacon and eggs,
Bacon and eggs,
Everybody here likes
Bacon and eggs.

We eat them all day,
Never throw them away,
We all like bacon and eggs.

Ice cream and eggs
Ice cream and eggs
Everyone here likes
Ice cream and eggs.

We eat them all day,
Never throw them away,
We all like ice cream and eggs.

Beans and eggs,
Beans and eggs,
Everyone here likes
Beans and eggs.

We eat them all day,
Never throw them away,
We all like beans and eggs.

Eggs and eggs,
Eggs and eggs,
Everyone here likes
Eggs and eggs.

We eat them all day,
Never throw them away,
We all like eggs and eggs.

Activities

- Use as a model to demonstrate how to write new verses for a performance poem.
- Focus on the rhythm and repetition of phrases.

Term 2
Non-fiction

Instructions Grandma's cottage
Main focus Drafting (see also pages 43 and 44)
NLS teaching objectives S9, S10, T16

Well now, let me think. If you want to get to my cottage from your house you'll need to go through the forest. Go into the forest through the old gate by the stream. Then you have to walk along the path that goes along by the stream. You might see some very pretty flowers on the bank of the stream but make sure you don't pick them because you're not allowed to. Then when you come to a fork in the path just past the old oak tree, go right. Keep going along that path until you see the little muddy pond. Be careful that you don't get your shoes dirty. You might be better wearing your wellies. Anyway, at the pond, turn left and go up the grassy lane. At the top of the lane you will see a little white gate. Go through the gate and make sure you shut it carefully behind you. Go up the garden path and knock at my blue front door. Knock loudly because I'm a little bit hard of hearing. Then we'll have some lemonade and biscuits.

Activities

- Discuss the purpose of directions.
- Focus on the lengthy sentences and delete all unnecessary words (i.e. adjectives, personal pronouns, unimportant detail).
- Demonstrate how to rewrite as impersonal directions.

- Use these directions to produce a map showing the route described in these directions.

Term 2
Non-fiction

Instructions Grandma's cottage
Main focus Model text (see also page 44)
NLS teaching objectives S9, S10, T16

How to get to Grandma's cottage

1 Go into the forest through the gate by the stream.

2 Walk along the path by the stream.

3 Go right at the fork in the path.

4 Turn left at the pond.

5 Go up the lane.

6 Go through the gate at the top of the lane.

7 Go up the garden path.

8 Knock loudly at the front door.

Activities

- Compare with page 42, discuss which words, phrases and details have been deleted.
- Focus on the use of the second person and the imperative voice.

- Replace the repeated verb 'Go' with appropriate alternatives.

Term 2
Non-fiction

Instructions Grandma's cottage
Main focus Model text (see also page 43)
NLS teaching objectives S9, S10, T16

How to get to Grandma's cottage ——————— Title

1 (Go) into the forest through the gate by the stream.

Verbs positioned at beginning of sentences. Present tense used

2 (Walk) along the path by the stream.

3 Go right at the fork in the path.

4 Turn left at the pond.

Sequential instructions 1 to 8

5 Go up the lane.

6 Go through the gate at the top of the lane.

7 Go up the garden path.

8 Knock loudly at the front door.

Activities

- Discuss which words, phrases and details have been deleted.
- Focus on the use of the second person and the imperative voice.

- Replace the repeated verb 'Go' with appropriate alternatives.

Term 3
Fiction

Adventure stories Rick, Lara and Scruffy
Main focus Detailed plan for episodes
NLS teaching objective T10

Characters

Two children, a boy and a girl, their new pet dog.
Lonely old man, his old pet dog has recently died.

Setting

Wet streets. Children walking the new puppy.
Old house where the lonely old man lives. It seems deserted.

Beginning

They are taking their new puppy out for a walk when it slips out of its collar and runs into the garden of a tumble-down old house, and they try to find it.

Problem

The boy, being brave, follows the dog through a gap in a door and vanishes into the house. Falls down some broken stairs and calls out for help. Scary old man appears in the garden and shouts to girl to go away.

Ending

Girl befriends old man, who helps take boy and pet dog home.

Activities

  • Model thought processes as you fill in some detail for the story plan.

  • Use the planning frame (see page 30) for shared/independent writing.

Term 3 Fiction

Adventure stories Rick, Lara and Scruffy
Main focus Improving a draft opening
NLS teaching objective T11

Rick and Lara went for a walk to the park with their new pet.

He was a puppy called Scruffy.

Suddenly he slipped out from his collar and ran into an old house.

'Come back bad dog', they shouted to him, but he didn't come back.

Activities

- Use this draft to discuss how adding detail can set the scene and mood effectively.
- Draft the next episode based on whole-class plan (see page 45).

- Write the next episode using own ideas.

Term 3 Fiction

Adventure stories Rick, Lara and Scruffy
Main focus Drafting (see also page 48)
NLS teaching objectives W13, S4, T11

Rick and Lara ran laughing along the wet pavement as they dashed towards Townly Park. This was the first time they had been allowed to take Scruffy out alone. He was old enough now, but still a really bouncy little puppy. They had wished for a dog for so long, and now their wish had come true.

Scruffy was as pleased as they were; he tugged on the lead, and barked joyfully to be out along the damp street. Suddenly he smelt something that excited him even more. There was a grassy, doggy smell. With a twist of his neck, he was free of his collar, and squeezing through the railings into the tangled garden of an old deserted house.

"Scruffy! Come back!" cried Lara, "Bad dog!" Rick and Lara stood, horrified, as they watched Scruffy scramble through a broken bit of door and disappear.

Activity

- Use as a model to demonstrate how to add descriptive detail, adjectives and adverbs to create a mental picture, and how to punctuate speech, etc.

Term 3 Fiction

Adventure stories Rick, Lara and Scruffy
Main focus Model text (see also page 47)
NLS teaching objectives W13, S4, T11

WHO

Adverb – HOW

Adverb – WHERE

(Rick and Lara) ran (laughing) along the (wet pavement) as they dashed towards Townly Park. This was the first time they had been allowed to take (Scruffy) out alone. He was old enough now, but still a really (bouncy little) puppy. They had wished for a dog for so long, and now their wish had come true.

Adjectives

Creates mood

(Scruffy was as pleased as they were;) he tugged on the lead, and barked (joyfully) to be out along the (damp) street. Suddenly he smelt something that excited him even more.

Adjective

Adverb

(There was a grassy, doggy smell.) With a twist of his neck, he was free of his collar, and squeezed through the railings into the tangled garden of an old deserted house.

Short sentence to increase pace

Speech punctuation

("Scruffy! Come back!") cried Lara, "Bad dog!" Rick and Lara stood, (horrified,) as they watched Scruffy scramble through a (broken bit) of door and (disappear.)

Alters mood

- Use as a model to demonstrate how to add descriptive detail, adjectives and adverbs to create a mental picture, and how to punctuate speech, etc.

48

Term 3 Fiction

Adventure stories Rick, Lara and Scruffy
Main focus Drafting (see also page 50)
NLS teaching objectives S2, S4, T12

I didn't know what to do. He had disappeared through the window after him. Come back, I called, come back Rick. But they didn't.

I followed him into the garden, and looked in through a window. An old man was sitting on a chair with Scruffy on his knee. I heard him say you look just like my old Tam.

I was frightened, but decided to speak to him. He's hurt. Will you help him? I said. Is he yours? asked the old man.

Activities

- Discuss how a first person account gives a different 'voice' and viewpoint.
- Identify the pronouns.
- Correct confusing pronouns/nouns for clarity.
- Add speech marks and place speech on new lines for different characters.

- Rewrite opening from a different point of view.

Term 3 Fiction

Adventure stories Rick, Lara and Scruffy
Main focus Model text (see also page 49)
NLS teaching objectives S2, S4, T12

I didn't know what to do. Rick had disappeared through the window after Scruffy.

"Come back, Rick," I called. "Scruffy, come back." But they didn't and I was left alone with no brother and no dog!

I decided I had to follow them into the garden, and crept through the long wet grass to the window. I peered through and saw an old man sitting on a chair with Scruffy on his knee.

"You look just like my old Tam," he sighed.

He looked old and dirty; I felt scared but I had to speak to him.

"My brother's hurt. Will you help him?" I pleaded.

"Is this dog yours?" asked the old man clutching Scruffy to his chest.

Activities

- Use as a model to show how first person accounts give a different viewpoint, how to use pronouns correctly and how to punctuate speech.

- Write the next episode.

Term 3 Fiction

Book reviews Model
Main focus Model text
NLS teaching objective T14

Title:	Grandpa Chatterji
Author:	Jamila Gavin
Illustrator:	Mei-Yum Low

Synopsis (Some detail about the story.)

Grandpa Chatterji comes to visit Neetu and Sanjay in England. They are not sure if they will like him, but he surprises them. They begin to see familiar things in a different way when they are with Grandpa Chatterji

Best or worst things:

The funniest part - Grandpa Chatterji puts floury handprints on Grandpa Leicester's suit while cooking pakoras.
The worst part is that the illustrations are not very exciting, but they are not important to the story.

Who will enjoy this book:

Both boys and girls will enjoy reading this book. Parents will like it also.

Star rating:

* * * * *

Activity

- Use this as a model book review. Draw attention to the brief nature of a synopsis and to the evaluation in the 'best or worst things' section.

Term 3 Fiction

Book reviews Planning frame
Main focus Drafting
NLS teaching objective T14

Title:
Author:
Illustrator:

Who is in it?

Where is it set?

What are the best and/or worst things about it?

Who would like reading it? Try to explain why.

How I rate it:
(5 stars = very good. 1 star = not good)

Activities

 • Use the planning frame to draft a book review.

 • Use the planning frame to draft a book review for a specified audience.

Term 3 Poetry

Language poems *The Wind* and *The Bay*
Main focus Improving a first draft (see also page 54)
NLS teaching objective T15

The Wind
The wind went wailing through the wood
With
Branches banging
Feathers fluttering
Twigs knocking

The Bay
A breeze brought sunshine to the bay
With
Sparkling sand
Crabs moving
Flying seagulls

Activity

- Focus on ineffective words (e.g. banging) and alliteration, and improve the draft.

Term 3 Poetry

Language poems *The Wind* and *The Bay*
Main focus Alliteration and onomatopoeia (see also page 53)
NLS teaching objective T15

The Wind
A wild wind went wailing through the wood
With . . .
Broken branches battering
Fluttering feathers flapping
Tapping twigs tangling

The Bay
A balmy breeze brought brightness to the bay
With . . .
Sparkling sands shimmering
Crusty crabs creeping
Soaring seagulls swooping

Activities

 • Use as a model text to illustrate alliteration and onomatopoeia.

 • Use different settings (e.g. the playground) to draft own versions.

Term 3
Non-fiction

Character portraits Our Class assembly about pets
Main focus Model (see also page 56)
NLS teaching objectives T22, T25

Who?

Our class, with Neeta, (and her frog called Geoffrey), Wayne, Mrs Mason, some policemen, Mr Deans.

What?

Neeta's frog escaped and hopped towards Mrs Mason. Mrs Mason jumped on to the piano stool. Wayne fell off the stage and banged into the stool. Mrs Mason fell off the stool and on to Geoffrey (the frog). Mr Deans tried to calm us all down. Some police came to see what the problem was.

When?

Today, during morning assembly.

Where?

Our school, in the hall.

Why?/Feeling?

It was our class assembly about pets. We had done lots of practice.
But afterwards Neeta was sad, Mrs Mason had hysterics, Mr Deans was angry. The rest of us thought it was very funny, except now we aren't allowed to take animals to school.

Activity

• Use to model how to organise the elements of a recount.

Term 3
Non-fiction

Recounts Planning frame
Main focus Making notes (see also page 55)
NLS teaching objectives T22, T25

Who?

What?

When?

Where?

Why?/Feeling?

Activities

- Use to structure own recounts.

- Use the planning frame to structure own recounts.

Term 3
Non-fiction

Recounts As a letter
Main Focus Model text
NLS teaching objectives S5, S6, T20, T22, T23

Dear Aunty Marge,

I know you'll be interested to hear how our class assembly went today. We had all practised very hard, so it is such a pity it went wrong.
We all stood in a row at the front, while the rest of the school came in to the hall in the dark. The curtains had been drawn so there was no light. When everyone was sitting down, the spotlight came on as planned, but it dazzled Neeta and she dropped Geoffrey, the frog. It ran straight at Mrs Mason, who screamed and jumped onto the piano stool.

Suddenly there was uproar. Some boys tried to catch the frog, and ran over to the piano. They knocked into Wayne, who fell backwards off the staging. He grabbed the school wall hanging and it fell over him.

He staggered around with it on his face, and our class began to laugh. It was so funny.

Meanwhile, Mrs Mason was still on the piano stool when Wayne crashed into her, knocking her on to the floor. Unfortunately she landed on the frog and squashed it. Then she screamed really loudly and everyone began to run out of the hall. Mr Deans shouted to be calm. However, some policemen suddenly burst into the hall.

Someone had heard all the noise and called the police! We aren't allowed to have live animals in assemblies any more. It is a shame, as I was going to take Monty, my python, next week.

Lots of love,

Sarah

Activities

- Draw attention to use of paragraphs and words that link paragraphs, phrases and clauses.

- Write the recount from a different viewpoint (e.g. Mrs Mason). Use paragraphs to structure writing.

Term 3
Non-fiction

Recounts As a newspaper report
Main focus Model text
NLS teaching objectives S5, S6, T22

Chaos in Local Primary School

Police were called to a scene of chaos at St Mary's School early on Monday, when a pet frog was killed.

Mrs Mason, who was responsible for squashing the frog when she fell off a piano stool, claimed it was an accident. She is still suffering from shock following the incident and is unavailable for comment.

The frog's owner, a pupil at St Mary's school, explained that she dropped the frog during a school assembly about pets.

Our reporter spoke later to the head teacher. He told us that a full investigation into the incident would take place, and gave assurances to the police officer on the scene that no more pets would suffer at his school.

Mrs Mason and the owner of the late frog have been offered counselling.

Activities

- Discuss the layout, the use of different typesizes, the sentence structure, impersonal voice, etc.

- Draft a letter from the headteacher to the school governors explaining what happened.

Term 3 Non-fiction

Recounts As a police report
Main focus Model text
NLS teaching objectives S5, S6, T22

At 09.15 hours on Monday, the duty sergeant received a report of a disturbance at St Mary's School.

Constable Duncan proceeded to the site of the disturbance. He found an animal had suffered grievous bodily harm at the hands of Mrs Mason, a teacher. The animal, a frog, was given all possible attention but failed to respond. It was pronounced dead by the local vet.

Constable Duncan cautioned Mrs Mason. The animal's owner decided not to press any charges, and no further action was taken.

Case closed. 10.00 hours.

Activity

- Discuss the sentence structure and the impersonal voice.

Term 3
Non-fiction

Recounts As a diary
Main focus Model text
NLS teaching objectives S5, S6, T22

<u>Monday</u>

Dear Diary,

Today Geoffrey died!!!

He was such a sweet little frog. If stupid Wayne hadn't banged into the piano, Geoffrey would still be alive.

I've buried him in the garden. Mum wouldn't let me cremate him!

I never got the chance to sing my song, 'A Frog can be your Friend' either. Mrs Mason said she was sorry for squashing him, but I don't believe her. She HATES frogs. I hate her!!!

I have decided to keep snails instead. At least they have shells to save them.

I'll write more tomorrow, I have to blow my nose now.

Neeta

Activities

- Discuss the sentence structure, tone and voice.
- Draw attention to the personal comments, informality and bias.